ISBN 978-1-330-22608-7
PIBN 10057506

This book is a reproduction of an important historical work. Forgotten Books uses state-of-the-art technology to digitally reconstruct the work, preserving the original format whilst repairing imperfections present in the aged copy. In rare cases, an imperfection in the original, such as a blemish or missing page, may be replicated in our edition. We do, however, repair the vast majority of imperfections successfully; any imperfections that remain are intentionally left to preserve the state of such historical works.

1 MONTH OF
FREE
READING

at
www.ForgottenBooks.com

By purchasing this book you are eligible for one month membership to ForgottenBooks.com, giving you unlimited access to our entire collection of over 700,000 titles via our web site and mobile apps.

To claim your free month visit:
www.forgottenbooks.com/free57506

The Dinner Party

WHEN you entertain, at dinner, without the help of servants, let the menu consist of dishes that may be prepared in advance and left a little while to keep cool, or warm as the case may be, without destroying their flavor. The first course may be on the table when the guests arrive, provided it is a fruit cocktail, or oysters or clams on the half shell.

A roast is a good choice for the second course; but have the gravy made and keeping hot in a double boiler; or else have a sauce such as mint or caper ready. If the green vegetable is peas, beans, asparagus or sprouts, it may be kept hot over hot water until the psychological moment. The best kind of potatoes would be those in a baking-dish or casserole. The accompanying jelly or pickles may be already in place on the table, or on the side table.

The salad should be in the ice-box carefully arranged on the plates and placed on a tray so that only one trip will be necessary. The dressing stands beside it ready to be added just before serving. The dessert should be one that requires no last-minute bustling about. A gelatine in a dainty mold can be turned out in advance and put in the ice-box. A lemon meringue pie is delicious and involves no trouble. Or perhaps a cold pudding will be the climax of the meal. If whipped cream or sauce is required, it too, may be ready ahead of time.

It is far more important for the hostess to be with her guests in the dining-room than preparing food in the kitchen. Her roles of cook and waitress should be as inconspicious as possible.

If coffee is to be the last on the menu, it should be ground and in the pot, ready to put on the stove between courses. Then it will be fresh and hot when it is needed. The coffee service may be ready on a tray in the pantry or on the sideboard or side table. Salted nuts and stuffed fruit or bonbons should also be ready.

Some Menus for Dinners

Beef Bouillon   Crisp Crackers
Roast Lamb with Brown Gravy
Peas ·   Mashed Brown Potatoes
Mint Jelly
Cheese Straws   Cucumber Salad with French Dressing
*Pistachio Ice-Cream
Salted Nuts   White Cakes
Coffee

_____

Clear Tomato Soup   Soup Sticks
Roast Chicken
String Beans   Sweet Potatoes
Sweet Pickles
Wafers   Hearts of Lettuce Salad and Russian Dressing
Chocolate Pie
Stuffed Figs   Coffee

_____

Fruit Cocktail
Fillet of Beef   Mushroom Sauce
Peas and Carrots   Baked Potatoes
Cream Pie
Stuffed Dates and Coffee

Clear Chicken Soup
Roast Beef   Toasted Saltines
Beets   Duchess Potatoes
Cold Slaw
Pineapple Salad and Cheese Crackers   Bavarian Cream
Cheese Dates   Yellow Sponge Cake
Coffee

Dinners for Special Occasions
Christmas or Thanksgiving Menus

Honey Dew Melons
*Halibut Turbans with Hollandaise Sauce and French Potato Balls
Roast Turkey with Stuffing and Gravy, Cranberry Sauce
Baked Onions   String Beans   White Potatoes
Celery
Red Apple Salad and Cheese Straws
Lemon, *Pumpkin or Mince Pie   *Plum Pudding with Foamy Sauce
Nuts and Raisins   Peppermints
Coffee   Grape Juice

Oysters on the Half Shell and Toaster Crackers
Chicken Pie
Beets   Parsnips   Squash   Mashed Potatoes
Sweet Pickle
Pineapple and Cream Cheese Salad with Wafers
Cranberry or Custard Pie
or
Thanksgiving Pudding with Hard Sauce
Salted Nuts   Stuffed Dates
Coffee   Fruit Punch

Oysters on the Half Shell
Roast Turkey with *Nut-Stuffing
Creamed Cauliflower   Baked Onions   Glazed Sweet Potatoes
Celery
*Frozen Cranberries
*Pecan and Grape Salad with Wafers
Apple or Pumpkin Pie
Nuts   Raisins
Coffee

Cream of Corn Soup with Popcorn Garnish
Stuffed Baked Fresh Ham
Mashed Brown Potatoes   Succotash
Cold Slaw   or   Sweet Pickles
*Filled Red Apple Salad with Cheese Straws
*Fig Pudding   Spiced Raisins
Coffee   Salted Butternuts

Easter Dinners

Spinach Soup   Egg-Yolk Garnish
                    Green Olives
Roast Capon   Potatoes with Parsley
Creamed Onions   Peas in Timbales
        *Water-Lily Salad and Cheese Ring
                *Topaz Ice
Cakes (spread with peanut butter and garnished
        with candied orange peel)
Salted Pecans   Coffee

Grape Fruit á la Violette
Saddle of Mutton with Mint and Currant Sauce
Quartered Brown Potatoes   String Beans
    Easter-Egg Salad and Crisped Rye Crackers
                        Cakes (frosted with maple
*Violet Ice   sugar and a candied
                        violet on each)
        Stuffed Dates   Coffee

Oyster Bouillon and Toasted Oatmeal Crackers
                    Radishes
Creamed Asparagus (in shells made of toasted bread)
            Broiled Fresh Salmon
New Green Cabbage   Duchess Potatoes
                Ripe Olives
    Romaine or Lettuce Salad and Corn Cuts
            Ginger Sherbet
*Angel Parfait   Pastry Fingers
                Coffee

Fish Dinners

*Fish Chowder
Fried Fish Steaks
Pickled Beets   String Beans
            Escalloped Potatoes
    Dressed Shrimps on Lettuce Leaves
            Grape-Juice Ice
Coffee   Plain Cookies

Salmon Soup
Baked Haddock with Tartare Sauce
Sweet Pickles   Mashed Brown Potatoes
Buttered Peas   Apple Pie and Cheese
            Coffee

Oyster Soup
Broiled Mackerel with Drawn-Butter Sauce
Potatoes au Gratin . Stewed Tomatoes
Dressed Lettuce with Sardine Garnish
Orange Jelly
Coffee Wafers

Simple Menus for Luncheons or Suppers

Broiled Lamb Chops
Creamed Potatoes and Peas
Hot French Biscuits Coffee

Scalloped Salmon Lima Beans
Toasted Cucumber Sandwiches
Coffee

Creamed Oysters French Fried Potatoes
Baked Stuffed Peppers
Cake Coffee

Cold Tongue or Ham Celery or Potato Salad
Sandwiches
Cocoa with Whipped Cream Cookies

Recipes for Novel Dinner-Dishes

HALIBUT TURBANS

A slice of halibut (1½ pounds) ⅛ teaspoonful pepper
¼ cupful melted butter or butter sub- 2 teaspoonfuls lemon juice
stitute Few drops onion juice
¼ teaspoonful salt

Clean fish and cut into 8 fillets. Add seasonings to melted butter. Take up each fillet with a fork, dip in butter, roll and fasten with a small wooden skewer. Put into a pan, dredge with flour and bake in a hot oven (20 minutes). Remove skewer and arrange on plate for serving. Garnish.

FISH CHOWDER

3 pounds cod or haddock 2 tablespoonfuls butter
2-inch cube fat salt pork 1 quart potato cubes
1 sliced onion ⅛ teaspoonful pepper
2 teaspoonfuls salt 1 quart hot milk

Have the fish skinned. Cut fish from backbone and divide in 2-inch pieces. Put head, backbone and tail in kettle with one quart cold water; heat slowly and cook about 30 minutes. Parboil potatoes for half an hour. Fry onion with pork. Strain fat into clean kettle. Put in fish and potatoes and over them strain the broth from the bones. Cook until potatoes are tender. Add seasoning, milk and crackers, if desired.

4

TURKEY STUFFING WITH NUTS

2 cupfuls nuts. If chestnuts, blanch and cook until tender and then put through a ricer. Walnuts may be chopped in the meat grinder.

4 tablespoonfuls fat	2 cupfuls bread crumbs moistened with
1 teaspoonful salt	4 tablespoonfuls butter
1 teaspoonful poultry seasoning	½ teaspoonful pepper

Melt the fat; mix all together. Moisten, if necessary for packing, with a little hot water.

FROZEN CRANBERRIES

4 cupfuls cranberries   2 cupfuls sugar
2 cupfuls boiling water

Pour the water over the sweetening, add the berries and cook 10 minutes. Cool. Put into a mold, cover tightly and pack in ice and salt for 4 hours. If preferred, the mixture may be strained before cooling. It may be frozen in a freezer by occasionally scraping the mixture from the sides and not turning it. Use equal partrs of ice and salt for packing.

GRAPE AND PECAN SALAD

Dip white grapes into water that has just stopped boiling for one-half minute; plunge into cold water. Skin, make a tiny opening and remove the seed. Put into a French dressing to marinate. Just before serving, drain, and insert, in the place of the seed, a tiny piece of pecan or other nut. Serve very cold on lettuce or romaine with a French dressing.

FILLED RED APPLE SALAD

Select firm red apples, and carefully remove the inside from the stem end, leaving a wall about one-quarter of an inch thick. Brush the inside with lemon juice and place in the ice-box. Chop the apple which came from the inside, after removing the core, and mix with an equal quantity with minced celery and a sprinkling of chopped nuts. Moisten with cream dressing, well seasoned, fill the apples and serve on lettuce. If desired, a slice can be cut from the top of the apple, carefully saved, and replaced when served. Otherwise, garnish with yellow celery tops.

WATER-LILY SALAD

Cook eggs hard and put into cold water to cool. Carefully remove shell and cut the eggs lengthwise. Remove yolks and mash with fork. Season and mix with salad dressing. Form into the center of the flowers. Cut the whites in narrow strips and lay them around the centers, forming petals of water-lily. Garnish with watercress, marinated in French dressing.

PUMPKIN PIE FILLING

Stew pumpkin with a little water; sift through a strainer. For each pie take

1 cupful pumpkin	1 egg
2 cupfuls milk	Sugar to taste
½ teaspoonful cinnamon	½ teaspoonful ginger

Grating of nutmeg

Mix all the ingredients and bake in a crust in a slow oven.

PLUM PUDDING

1 pound raisins	8 eggs
1 pound currants	½ pound flour
¼ pound candied orange peel	½ pound brown sugar
½ pound citron	1 nutmeg grated
½ pound chopped suet	1 tablespoonful cinnamon
½ pound stale bread crumbs	¼ tablespoonful allspice

½ pint grape juice

Wash and dry the currants. Cut citron and orange peel very fine. Stone raisins. Mix all dry ingredients together. Beat eggs; pour them over the dry ingredients, add the liquid and mix thoroughly. Pack into greased molds, and steam 4 hours at time of making, and reheat when wanted for use. Serve with hard sauce.

FIG PUDDING

1 pound chopped figs	3 eggs
1 cupful suet	1 teaspoonful cinnamon
1 pint fine bread crumbs	1 teaspoonful nutmeg
½ cupful sugar	½ cupful grape juice or jelly

Beat eggs well. Mix the dry ingredients. Combine with the other ingredients. Steam 3 hours. Serve with hard sauce made with brown sugar to which a tablespoonful of cream has been slowly added.

PISTACHIO ICE-CREAM

2 cupfuls scalded milk	1 egg
1 tablespoonful flour	½ teaspoonful salt
1 cupful sugar	1 quart thin cream
1 tablespoonful vanilla	1 teaspoonful almond

Mix flour, sugar and salt; add egg slightly beaten, and milk gradually. Cook as a soft custard. When cool add cream and flavoring; strain and color green with vegetable coloring. Freeze.

TOPAZ ICE

1 can apricots	2 cupfuls water
1 cupful sugar	2 cupfuls ginger ale

Juice of 2 lemons

Rub the apricots through a coarse sieve. Make a sirup of the water and sugar; boil 10 minutes. Cool. Add the other ingredients and freeze. Garnish with candied orange peel if desired. A pretty dessert for a "yellow" party.

VIOLET ICE

2 cupfuls grape juice	Juice of 2 lemons
4 cupfuls water	2 cupful sugar

½ ounce of citron, cut very fine

Make a sirup of the water and sugar and boil 10 minutes. Cool. Add the other ingredients and freeze. Grape jelly may be used and part of the sugar omitted. Melt the jelly and add to the hot sirup. Pretty for tea parties also.

ANGEL PARFAIT

1 cupful sugar	1 tablespoonful vanilla
½ cupful water	White of 3 eggs

1 pint cream

Boil the sugar and water until it spins a thread. Beat the white of the eggs until stiff, letting the sugar cool while you do the beating. Pour the sirup slowly into the whites, stirring all the time. Beat until the mixture is cool, add the cream and vanilla and freeze.

Luncheons or Suppers for Special Occasions

Lincoln's Birthday

Cream-of-Carrot Soup
Escalloped Oysters
Corn Gems   Lima Beans
Sweet Cucumber Pickles
Cottage Cheese Salad and Brown Bread Sandwiches
*Hot Apple Cake
Salted Butternuts   Maple Hard Sauce
Coffee

Saint Valentine's Day

Hearts of Lettuce with
Rye Wafers and Russian Dressing
Creamed Sweetbreads
Buttered Peas   Heart Sandwiches
Sour Pickles
Molded Ice-Cream (hearts and arrows)
Pistachio Nuts   Oatmeal Macaroons
Tea or Coffee

Washington's Birthday

*Cherry Cocktail
Maryland Chicken
Brussels Sprouts   Glazed Sweet Potatoes
Crabapple Jelly
Red Cabbage Salad and Cheese Straws
*Washington Pie
Salted Nuts   Coffee

Cool Menus for Summer Dinners and Luncheons

Jellied Chicken Soup
*Stuffed Airplane Tomatoes
Whole Wheat Bread   Cream Cheese
Strawberry Mold

Wheat Rolls Filled with Chicken Salad
Iced Tea   Bar-le-Duc Preserves
Floating Island   Raisin Cookies

---

*Stuffed Baked Cucumbers
Cold Sliced Meat   Brown-Bread Sandwiches
Pickles
*Fresh Fruit Ice-Cream   Spiced Cakes

Cold Tuna-Fish Timbales   Cream Dressing
Lettuce Sandwiches   Potato Chips
Pineapple Bracts   Coconut Cake
Ginger Ale

Baked Ham   Potato Salad
                Sliced Beets in Vinegar
            Shrimp Salad and Cheese Straws
        Raspberry   Ice Wafers
_____

            Meat Loaf   Buttered Peas
            Rice Biscuits   Iced Cocoa
        Orange Tapioca   Nut Cookies
_____

                Cold Tomato Bouillon
                *Green Corn Puffs
        Molded Rice (cooked in milk)   Mint Jelly
                Asparagus Salad
                Spanish Cream
_____

                Chilled Fruit Cocktail
        Cold Roast Beef   Young Green Onions
                Creamed New Potatoes
                Fruit Sherbet and Ladyfingers
                    Iced Coffee
_____

                Lobster Salad
        Brown-Bread Sandwiches   Coffee
                    Cantaloup
_____

                Chilled Watermelon
                Cold Chicken
        Boiled Corn   Potato Salad
                Peach Shortcake
                Iced or Hot Coffee
_____

                Cold Boiled Salmon
        Cucumbers   New Buttered Potatoes
            Half Cantaloups filled with Ice-Cream
                Grape Juice

Recipes for Special Luncheon Dishes

AIRPLANE TOMATOES

Select uniform small tomatoes, skin and chill. Take out the inside carefully and cut two slits on one side of the tomato and then two slits directly opposite; insert thin slices of cucumber in the slits. The tomatoes should be filled with well-seasoned chopped meat or flaked fish; left-over meats may be used.

STUFFED BAKED CUCUMBERS

Peel small cucumbers; cut a slice from the top and scoop out the inside. Fill with chopped meat or fish mixed with cooked rice and seasoned well. Sprinkle the top with buttered crumbs of stale bread. Bake until the cucumber is soft and the crumbs brown. Be sure to grease the baking dish before putting the cucumber on to bake. Serve with drawn-butter sauce flavored with lemon.

GREEN CORN PUFFS

2 eggs beaten stiff   Grated cheese
1 cupful milk   ½ teaspoonful paprika
1 pint grated corn   ½ teaspoonful salt
                Few grains cayenne

8

Beat two eggs until light. Add one cupful sweet milk, one pint grated corn, add salt and pepper. Grease well six custard cups. Fill them half full of mixture and place in a large cooking utensil which has been filled with hot water. Add one tablespoonful grated cheese to each cup. Bake in a moderate oven until firm. These puffs are much improved if served with tomato sauce.

APPLE CAKE

2 cupfuls flour	½ cupful fat
4 teaspoonfuls baking-powder	1 egg
½ teaspoonful salt	¾ cupful milk

Sift the dry ingredients, cut in the fat and add the egg well-beaten and the milk. Having ready sour apples pared, cored and cut in eighths; place in rows overlapping each other on the apple cake. Bake in a square tin in a hot oven until the apples are soft. Sprinkle with sugar and cinnamon before baking, if desired. Serve hot with maple hard sauce.

CHERRY COCKTAIL

This may be made from red or white canned cherries. Stone the cherries and drain from the liquid. If very sweet, add lemon juice enough to give a tart taste. Chill in the ice-box. Serve in a high glass and sprinkle with shredded coconut. Grapefruit may be combined with the cherries if desired.

WASHINGTON PIE

½ cupful fat	½ cupful milk
¾ cupful sugar	1½ cupfuls flour
2 eggs	2½ teaspoonfuls baking-powder
½ teaspoonful vanilla or ½ teaspoonful lemon extract	

Cream the fat, add the sugar gradually, then the eggs well-beaten. Add the flour in which the baking-powder has been sifted, alternately with the milk. Lastly add the flavoring. Bake in two layers in a round tin; fill with raspberry jam and sift sugar over the top.

FRESH FRUIT ICE-CREAM

2 cupfuls fruit juice or 3 cupfuls crushed fruit	1 quart cream
	2 cupfuls sugar

Crush the fruit, add sugar, allow to stand until sugar is dissolved. Scald one-half the cream, cool, combine all ingredients. Freeze. For frozen or water ice, use water instead of cream, adding 2 tablespoonfuls lemon juice.

Buffet Suppers

SUNDAY night is the time when guests may drop in unexpectedly and one should always plan what can serve more than "just the family."

A main dish with some kind of bread (generally hot), jelly, pickles or conserve, may comprise the first course; some dessert with cakes, cookies, or wafers is sufficient to serve for the second. If you have a chafing dish, now is the time to use it.

Much may be done in advance. The cake may be baked, the meat cooked ready to slice, the ingredients for the salad be ready in the ice-box and the dressing made; a dessert may be prepared the day before, or simple cookies may be baked.

Supper Menus with Meat

*Creamed Chicken with Pimientos
Olives
Brown-Bread Sandwiches (lettuce filling)

| Raspberry Gelatine | *Marshmallow Sauce |
| Nut Cakes | Tea with Lemon |

| Cold Sliced Meat | Grape Jelly |
| Cucumber Salad | Hot Corn Muffins |

Chocolate Layer Cake
Coffee

Supper Menus with Fish

*Manhattan Shrimps

| Toasted Bread | Sweet Pickle |

Strawberry Turnovers
Tea with Lemon

| Shad Roe Sauté | Nut Bread |

Cucumbers, Cream Dressing

| White Sponge Cake | *French Chocolate |

Supper Menus without Fish or Meat

*French Cinamon Toast
Orange Marmalade

| Cocoa with Marshmallows | Fresh Fruit Compote |

· Rice Wafers

Nut and Cottage-Cheese Salad

| Toasted Crackers | Mustard Pickles |
| *Fruit Short Cake | Tea |

Recipes for Some of the Supper Dishes

CREAMED CHICKEN WITH PIMIENTO

3 cupfuls cold cooked chicken cut in dice, or 1 one-pound can of chicken cut fine.

2½ cupfuls milk	⅛ teaspoonful pepper
5 tablespoonfuls flour	5 tablespoonfuls fat
1 pimiento cut in tiny pieces	1 teaspoonful salt

½ teaspoonful celery salt

Scald milk. Melt fat, add flour and seasoning and milk slowly. When thick, add chicken, and cook long enough to heat the chicken. Add pimiento last.

MANHATTAN SHRIMPS

1 pint of shrimps, canned or fresh	1 teaspoonful lemon juice
4 tablespoonfuls fat	1 tablespoonful flour
½ teaspoonful salt	1 cupful milk
Little cayenne	Yolk of 2 eggs

Clean the shrimp, and cook in half the fat for 2 minutes; add seasoning and lemon; cook 2 minutes longer. Remove shrimps and make a white sauce of the remaining fat, flour and milk; when thickened add yolks of eggs, slightly beaten, stirring in quickly and cooking 2 minutes; add the shrimps.

FRENCH CINNAMON TOAST

2 eggs	1 tablespoonful sugar
1 cupful of milk	1 teaspoonful salt
¾ teaspoonful cinnamon	6 slices bread

Beat the eggs a little, add salt, sugar and milk. Dip the toast in the mixture, drain, sprinkle with a little cinnamon; fry in a hot pan until a delicate brown. Serve with sirup.

MARSHMALLOW SAUCE

¼ pound marshmallows	½ teaspoonful vanilla
1 cupful powdered sugar	½ cupful boiling water

Melt marshmallows in top of double boiler. Stir sugar into boiling water until dissolved; add slowly to melted marshmallows and stir until thoroughly blended. Chill. Add vanilla. For variety, ½ cupful chopped pecan nuts or 6 minced candied cherries or 2 tablespoonfuls of finely shopped citron may be added.

FRENCH CHOCOLATE

Pour 1 pint boiling water over 4 tablets of sweet chocolate, cook slowly ½ hour. Add 1 pint scalded milk, and cook 15 minutes. Add 1 teaspoonful arrowroot starch mixed with ½ cupful cold water, and cook 10 minutes. Add 1 teaspoonful vanilla just before serving. The arrowroot may be omitted.

FRUIT SHORTCAKE

1-2/3 cupfuls flour	2 teaspoonfuls sugar
1/3 cupful potato flour	¾ cupful milk
4 tablespoonfuls fat	½ teaspoonful salt
4 teaspoonfuls baking powder	

Mix and sift the dry ingredients; cut in fat; add milk; roll out on floured board and cut into biscuit about one inch thick. Bake in hot oven. Split and cover lower part with stewed fruit, place upper part on top with crust side down, cover with fruit. This makes individual serving. The cake may be baked in one round piece, split and filled with fruit.

Afternoon Tea

TEA should be made from freshly drawn, boiling water and in an earthenware pot, so as not to be affected by acid, and one that will retain the heat. After the water is poured on, the pot should stand where it will keep very hot, but never boil, and the tea should be allowed to infuse three to five minutes. If you are not ready to use it at once, pour it off into a hot pot and keep it very hot.

If strong tea is made, have at hand boiling water in a hot water kettle to weaken the tea to suit individual tastes. If you use a tea-ball, do not fill it too full, for the tea must have room in which to swell in order to infuse properly.

Tea usually is served with thin slices of lemon or orange, with the seeds removed. Sometimes a piece of pineapple or strawberry is added to each cup. Or for variety, a tiny piece of vanilla bean is put into the tea pot. Often clove is used, several cloves being stuck in each piece of lemon. In serving, the fruit may be put directly in the cup but the loaf sugar should be placed on a saucer.

For the hot months, tea is better iced and served with cracked ice in tall glasses; put a bunch of fresh mint in the pitcher or a tiny spray in the top of each glass.

Dainty, delicious sandwiches can be made with various fillings. Little baking-powder biscuits cut with an oval cutter are very attractive. These should be buttered in the kitchen and served very hot. They may be brought in on a sandwich plate or in a Japanese bread basket lined with a plain doily. Little cakes, wafers, cookies or pastries are dainty sweets. For special occasions nuts or stuffed dates, prunes or raisins may be added.

The butter for sandwiches should always be creamed before spreading to make it go farther and spread more easily. Certain kinds of sandwiches are especially delicious if the slices of bread are spread with mayonaise or cooked salad dressing. All filling should be moist enough to spread easily, but not so moist as to soak the bread. Meat sandwiches should have the filling chopped or shaved, or cut in very thin slices. Fish should be flaked. Both must be well seasoned.

Sandwich-bread for an afternoon tea or reception should be sliced as thinly as possible and cut in fancy shapes. For lunches, the bread may be cut one-fourth inch thick. When the sandwiches are served they may be piled one above the other to keep from drying. A garnish of watercress is particularly appetizing.

Suggestions for Sandwich-Fillings

Baked beans mashed and mixed with salad dressing.

Flaked salmon with chopped cucumber (drain carefully); seasonings and salad dressing.

Chopped peanuts with jelly or banana-pulp, scraped. One banana to 1/4 cupful peanuts.

Minced celery, chopped pineapple, seasonings, and cooked dressing.

Cooked fig paste and marshmallows. Melt the marshmallows in a double boiler and combine with the fig paste.

Prune or apricot pulp, lemon juice, and chopped nuts or raisins.

Preserved ginger, chopped nuts, lemon juice and sirup from the ginger, to moisten.

Orange marmalade or jellies.

Hard-cooked eggs chopped fine, seasoned with salt, pepper and a speck of mustard, oil and vinegar, and a finely-minced green or red pepper.

Mayonnaise with lettuce, watercress or other salad plant, or finely-chopped olives (well-seasoned).

Cream cheese seasoned with finely-chopped nuts.

Recipes for Unusual Delights at Tea

SWEET PASTRY

2 cupfuls flour	3/4 cupful fat (butter preferred)
1/2 cupful brown sugar	1/2 teaspoonful salt

Mixed the flour and sugar. Cut in the fat, very fine. Roll on a floured pastry-board until the dough is about 1/2 inch thick; cut out with fancy cutters. Bake in a slow oven. Brush or mark with beaten yolk of egg mixed with 1/4 teaspoonful water just before the pastries are done.

CHOCOLATES

Use the above mixture or a recipe for pastry. Cut one piece with a round cutter and then one the same size with a doughnut cutter. Bake, and put together with crocolate frosting. Cover with the frostings, putting a little in the center. Sprinkle with pistachio or other nuts.

TEA CAKES

2 cupfuls flour	4 teaspoonfuls baking-powder
½ teaspoonful salt	4 tablespoonfuls fat
2/3 cupful milk	Candied cherries, raisins, nuts, or candied fruit, cut in pieces

Sift dry ingredients, and cut in fat; add the milk. Roll on a floured board and cut into tiny biscuits about as large as a quarter. On top of each, put a candied cherry, a raisin, a nut or a piece of candied fruit. Brush over with melted fat, and bake in a hot oven. The inside of an old doughnut cutter makes a good cutter for these biscuits if a small cutter cannot be had; or use the top of a small can, making a few holes in the top to let out the air as you press down to cut the biscuit.

These cakes need not be served with butter, as they are very rich.

CHEESE BISCUIT

2 cupfuls flour	Yolk of 1 egg
½ teaspoonful salt	4 teaspoonfuls baking-powder
2/3 cupful milk	2 tablespoonfuls fat
½ cupful grated cheese	

Mix and sift dry ingredients. Beat the yolk, add it·to the milk, and pour slowly into the dry ingredients. Roll out ½ inch thick on a floured board. Place one of the biscuits on a baking-sheet and cover it with a thin layer of the cheese; place another on the top and sprinkle a little of the cheese on that. Bake in a quick oven. If the egg-yolk is very large, less milk may be used.

COFFEE BISCUIT

2 cupfuls flour	2/3 cupful strong coffee
½ teaspoonful salt	4 teaspoonfuls baking-powder
3 teaspoonfuls sugar	3 tablespoonfuls fat
½ cupful raisins	

Mix and sift dry ingredients, and cut in fat; add raisins and coffee. Roll out and cut into biscuits, brush over top with milk and bake in a hot oven about 15 minutes.

The prepared coffees on the market make excellent coffee for this recipe.

CREAM SCONES

2 cupfuls flour	1/3 cupful cream
1 tablespoonful sugar	4 teaspoonfuls baking-powder
4 tablespoonfuls fat	½ teaspoonful salt
2 eggs	

Sift dry ingredients. Cut in fat. Beat eggs and add them to cream. Pour into dry ingredients, mixing with a kinfe. Toss on a floured board and roll out about ¾ inch thick. Cut with a sharp knife into squares or diamond shapes and bake in a hot oven for 15 minutes.

Bridal Breakfasts

FOR a large reception the buffet style of serving is the only one to use. Let each lady's escort serve her and himself with a plate, and in this way, with the help of the caterer's men, the confusion of getting refreshments to the guests will be lessened. When the post-wedding party is small, a group of the bride's friends can assist at the affair.

Table decorations play a large part in the effectiveness of a seated breakfast or supper. Roses and sweet peas are June flowers that decorate deligthfully. Place cards and favors give delicate color tone to the table.

For the announcement supper or wedding breakfast a few well-chosen, daintily served foods are better by far than are elaborate repast. It may be advisable to call upon your caterer for the ice-creams and for some of the fancy cakes, but the menus given here may be prepared at home.

Bridal Breakfast Menus

Strawberry Cocktail

Molded Chicken Salad   Cold Sliced Tongue
Parker House Rolls   Sweet Pickles
Caramel Bavarian
Sponge Cakes   Nut Sauce
Coffee Bon Bons

Bouillon   Wafers
*Salmon Cutlets with New Peas
Broiled Squab
Rolls   French Fried Potatoes
Orange and Cherry Salad with Cheese Straws
Charlotte Russe
Sponge Sticks Glazed Nuts
Coffee

Consommé en Tasse
Cold Boned Chicken in Aspic Sauce Tartare
Creamed Asparagus in Patty Shells
Bread Sticks   Olives
Strawberry Ice-Cream
*Bride's Cake Macaroons
Coffee

Wedding Breakfasts and Announcement Luncheons

Grapefruit Stuffed with White Grapes
*Halibut Turbans with Hollandaise Sauce
*Chicken à la King Hot Rolls
Lettuce and Celery Salad Cheese Straws
Vanilla and Pistachio Ice-Cream
*Bride's Cake Coffee

Cream of Watercress Soup in Cups
Olives   Crackers
Timbale Cases filled with Creamed Fish
Cold Chicken and Tongue Assorted Sandwiches
Tomato-and-Cucumber Salad
Strawberry Shortcake
Coffee

Tomato Bouillon
Cold Ham and Chicken
Hot Rolls   Currant Jelly
Hot Creamed Asparagus
Bread and Butter Sandwiches
Strawberry or Lemon Ice
(served in meringues)
Almond Macaroons   Sponge Cakes
Coffee   Glazed Walnuts and Pecans

Strawberries au Naturel
*Ham Mousse
Buttered Peas   New Potatoes in Cream
Cherry Tarts
Coffee   Salted Nuts

SALMON CUTLETS

2 cupfuls cold flaked salmon (or 1 can)   3 tablespoonfuls fat
1 cupful milk   ½ teaspoonful pepper
1 teaspoonful lemon juice   4 tablespoonfuls flour
1 teaspoonful salt

Make a white sauce of the milk, flour and fat, add the seasonings, then the salmon and lemon. Chill. Form into the shape of cutlets, egg and crumb and fry in deep fat. Insert a piece of macaroni for the bone and finish with a paper frill. The sauce must be cooked until very thick. Be careful not to let it burn.

HALIBUT TURBANS (See page 4)

CHICKEN À LA KING

2 tablespoonfuls fat   3½ cupfuls cooked chicken cut fine
2 tablespoonfuls flour   2 tablespoonfuls fat
½ teaspoonful salt   Yolks 2 eggs
1 pint fresh milk or cream   1 tablespoonful lemon juice
6 fresh mushroom caps   Few drops onion juice
1 green or red sweet pepper cut fine   ½ teaspoonful paprika

Peel the mushroom caps and cut fine. Cook with the pepper in the first quantity of fat for three minutes. Remove the mushrooms and pepper and add the flour and milk. Cook until you have a boiling mixture; add the chicken, pepper and mushrooms. Put into the top of a double boiler. Cream the second quality of fat and stir in the egg yolks and seasoning; add to the chicken mixture and cook until the egg yolks are cooked, stirring constantly.

HAM MOUSSE

2 cupfuls boiled ham minced very fine   ½ cupful whipped cream
1 tablespoonful gelatine softened in 2   ½ teaspoonful paprika
  tablespoonfuls cold water   Few grains cayenne
½ cupful boiling water   1 tablespoonful finely minced parsley

Pour the hot water on the softened gelatine; add the ham, seasonings and the cream; mix thoroughly and mold in individual molds or a large mold. Serve, garnished with parsley.

BRIDE'S CAKE

¼ cupful butter
1½ cupfuls sugar
1 cupful milk
½ teaspoonful cream of tartar

2½ cupfuls flour
3 teaspoonfuls baking-powder
½ teaspoonful almond extract
Whites of 6 eggs

Cream butter; add sugar, gradually, and continue beating. Mix and sift the flour, baking-powder and cream of tartar, and add alternately with the milk to the first mixture. Add extract. Beat the whites of the eggs until stiff and add last. Bake about 45 minutes.

Children's Parties

ICE-CREAM, of which nothing else can take the place at a child's party, has been planned in nearly all of the following menus. These refreshments are simply prepared and suitable for children between the ages of five and twelve years.

Menus for Children's Parties

Sandwiches with Peanut-Butter and Chopped Raisin Filling
Sandwiches filled with Currant Jelly
Cocoa   Animal Cookies
*Basket Ice-Cream
Lollypops

Creamed Chicken
White and Brown-Bread Sandwiches
*Orange Ice-Cream (in orange shells)
Stick Candy Ladies   Fancy Cakes

Raspberry Shrub
Honey Sandwiches of Graham and White Bread
Catawba Grape Juice
*Chocolate Charlotte
Molasses Chips   Sponge Cakes

Cold Chicken and Tongue
Date and Fig Sandwiches   Baking-Powder Biscuit
Cocoa with Marshmallow
*Caramel Ice-Cream
Oat Macaroons
Little Cakes
Barley Sugar and Chocolate Animals

For Very Little Tots

Graham Crackers
Zweibach
Cooked Prune or Banana Pulp
Tapioca Cream
Plain Cookies   Milk

16

Recipes for Sweets for Children's Parties

BASKET ICE-CREAM

Make small plain cakes and take out the inside. Put in a teaspoonful of jam or sweet jelly and then a ball of vanilla ice-cream. Make the handle of the basket of citron cut in strips, or angelica.

ORANGE ICE-CREAM

2 cupfuls sugar	1 cupful milk
1 cupful water	Yolks 2 eggs
2 cupfuls orange juice	1 cupful thick cream

Boil the sugar and water 8 minutes slowly. Add the orange juice after cooling. Make a custard of the milk and egg yolks. Strain, cool and add to the first mixture. Beat the cream and add it. Freeze. If desired, 1/4 cupful candied orange peel, cut fine, may be added to the ice-cream when nearly frozen.

CHOCOLATE CHARLOTTE

1/2 cupful boiling water	1/4 cupful cold water
1/4 cupful sugar	1/4 cupful cream (scalded)
1 1/4 cupfuls cream	1 1/2 squares chocolate
1 1/4 tablespoonfuls gelatine	Vanilla

Soak the gelatine in cold water. Add the scalded cream to it while hot. Stir until gelatine is dissolved. Melt the chocolate over hot water, add the sugar slowly and then the boiling water a little at a time. Add slowly to the gelatine mixture while both are hot. Cool. Add the cream to 1 teaspoonful vanilla. Pour into a fancy mold lined with lady fingers.

CARAMEL ICE-CREAM

2 cupfuls scalded milk	1 cupful sugar
1/4 cupful sugar	1/4 cupful boiling water
3 eggs	1 quart thin cream
1/2 tablespoonful salt	2 teaspoonfuls vanilla

Make a custard of the first four ingredients, strain and cool. Caramelize 1 cupful of sugar and add boiling water to it. Cool. Combine mixtures, add cream and vanilla. Freeze.

McCall's Service

Spending The Family Income: Why True Economy Means Living by a Plan. What a plan of expenditures includes—percentage of income to apportion for shelter, food, clothing, operating expenses, development, savings.   10 cents

A Group of Little Homes. Compiled by Robert Cummings Wiseman, from plans designed by expert small-house architects. Twelve houses, with complete architectural plans.   10 cents

The Modern Home: How to Equip it with Mechanical Servants and Manage it Wisely. By Lillian Purdy Goldsborough. Labor-saving devices and methods to do the housework in a servantless home.   10 cents

Down the Garden Path. By Dorothy Giles, member of The Garden Club of America. Practical directions for flower and vegetable gardening.   10 cents

Time-Saving Cookery. Prepared by The House of Sarah Field Splint. Menus and recipes all specially originated for McCall readers, indicating how package and canned foods, bought at the neighborhood grocery, can be used to supply delightful, well-balanced, wholesome meals, and at the same time spare the home-cook both time and work.   10 cents

Master-Recipes: A New Time-Saving Method in Cookery. Ten recipes given in one for making gelatin desserts, soufflés, muffins, cream-sauce dishes, cream soups, sauces for meat or fish, custards, bread puddings, bavarian creams, ices, cakes, cookies, doughnuts, cake frostings, candies.   10 cents

What to Serve at Parties. Compiled by Lilian M. Gunn, Department of Foods and Cookery, Teacher's College, Columbia University, from her articles previously published in McCall's. Menus and special recipes for Luncheons, Dinners, Teas, Suppers, Bridal Breakfasts and Children's Parties.   10 cents

Parties All The Year. One for every month. By Claudia M. Fitzgerald. Suggestions for rhymed invitations, games, contest, stunts, costumes, prizes, refreshments.   10 cents

More Parties. By Claudia M. Fitzgerald.   10 cents

Entertaining Without a Maid. By Edna Sibley Tipton. Correct Table Service for Breakfast Parties, Luncheons, Teas, Receptions, Dinners, Sunday Night Suppers.   10 cents

The Bride's Own Book. Suggestions for Formal and Informal Weddings in the Church and in the Home.   10 cents

A Book of Manners. The etiquette of introduction, calls, invitations, gifts, manners at table and in public places, fees, funerals and mourning, correspondence, childrens' manners, and so forth.   10 cents

The Friendly Mother: A Book of Prenatal Mothercraft. Written by Helen Johnson Keyes and approved by Franklin A. Dorman, M. D., Head of the Maternity Division of The Woman's Hospital, New York City. A guide for the young mother during the long months before her baby comes.   10 cents

To get the booklets, address (enclosing postage) The Service Editor, McCall's Magazine, 236 West 37th Street, New York City.

CPSIA information can be obtained
at www.ICGtesting.com
Printed in the USA
BVHW041213281218
536599BV00014B/485/P